D1537655

Animal Look-Alikes
Wolves and Coyotes

Joanne Mattern

RED
CHAIR
• PRESS •

Animal Look-Alikes is produced and published by Red Chair Press:

Red Chair Press LLC   PO Box 333   South Egremont, MA 01258-0333

www.redchairpress.com

About the Author

Joanne Mattern is the author of nearly 350 books for children and teens. She began writing when she was a little girl and just never stopped! Joanne loves nonfiction because she enjoys bringing science topics to life and showing young readers that nonfiction is full of compelling stories! Joanne lives in the Hudson Valley of New York State with her husband, four children, and several pets, which look nothing alike!

Publisher's Cataloging-In-Publication Data
Names: Mattern, Joanne, 1963-
Title: Wolves and coyotes / Joanne Mattern.

Description: [South Egremont, Massachusetts] : Red Chair Press, [2018] | Series: Animal look-alikes | Interest age level: 006-010. | Includes science vocabulary, fun facts, and trivia about each type of animal. | "Core content library." | Includes bibliographical references. | Summary: "Thick fur. Thin face or wide face. Long howls or short yips. Is it a wolf or a coyote? Learn how these beautiful wild creatures are alike and how they differ."--Provided by publisher.

Identifiers: LCCN 2017934020 | ISBN 978-1-63440-291-0 (library hardcover) | ISBN 978-1-63440-292-7 (ebook)

Subjects: LCSH: Wolves--Juvenile literature. | Coyote--Juvenile literature. | CYAC: Wolves. | Coyote.

Classification: LCC QL737.C22 M38 2018 (print) | LCC QL737.C22 (ebook) | DDC 599.77--dc23

Illustrations by Tim Haggerty.

Illustrations p. 7, 22 by Joe LeMonnier.

Photo credits: Shutterstock.

Printed in Canada

102017 1P FRNS18

Table of Contents

Wolf or Coyote?

Ah-oooh! You hear a strange howl in the dark. Then you see a big furry animal looking into the night sky. The animal turns to look at you, then runs away. Was this animal a wolf? Or was it a coyote? Or maybe it was a dog!

Wolves and coyotes—and dogs—look a lot alike. Sometimes they act alike too. But they are different **species** of animals. How can you tell these animals apart? Let's find out the differences between wolves and coyotes.

A Family Divided

Wolves and coyotes are both part of the same family. That family is the **canine** family. Dogs are part of this family too. So are foxes and jackals.

Red fox

About two million years ago, the canine family split into two groups. One group was called vulpine. The vulpine group included foxes. The other group was called lupine. The lupine group included wolves and coyotes. About one million years ago, wolves and coyotes split into two different species.

Power Word: Lupine means showing features like a wolf. Vulpine means having features more like a fox: smaller and clever.

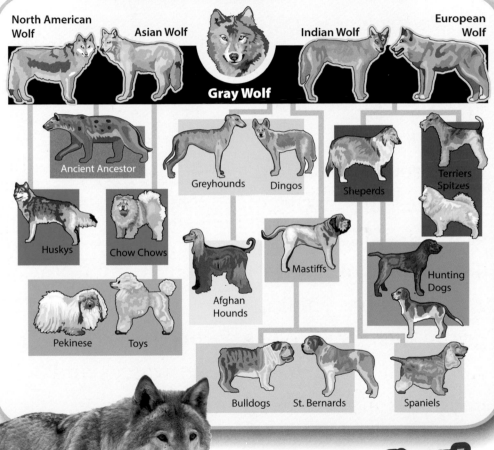

North American Wolf

Asian Wolf

Gray Wolf

Indian Wolf

European Wolf

Ancient Ancestor

Greyhounds

Dingos

Sheperds

Terriers
Spitzes

Huskys

Chow Chows

Mastiffs

Hunting Dogs

Afghan Hounds

Pekinese

Toys

Bulldogs

St. Bernards

Spaniels

Now You Know!

Scientists think that long, long ago, people domesticated wolves and turned them into pet dogs.

Coats of Many Colors

Wolves and coyotes are both mammals. Mammals are warm-blooded. They can control their body temperature. Their bodies stay the same temperature no matter what the temperature is around them. This is helpful, because some mammals live where it is very hot. Some live where it is very cold.

A mammal's body is covered with fur or hair. Fur is one way you can tell wolves and coyotes apart. A wolf's fur is usually darker than a coyote's fur. Wolves can be dark gray or black. Some wolves are reddish-brown. Coyotes are usually light brown or pale gray.

Now You Know!

The most common species of wolf is the gray wolf.

Eurasian wolf

Coyote

Wolf snout

Coyote snout

Big and Not So Big

Size is another way to tell wolves and coyotes apart. Wolves are bigger than coyotes. A male gray wolf can weigh between 66 and 180 pounds (30 to 82 kg). Females weigh between 50 and 120 pounds (23 to 55 kg). They measure between three and five feet (1 to 1.5 m) long.

Coyotes are a lot smaller. They weigh between 15 and 46 pounds (6.5 to 21 kg) and are about two-and-a-half feet (0.75m) long. As with wolves, females are smaller than males.

A wolf's head is also bigger than a coyote's head. A wolf's snout is wide. A coyote's snout is thinner and more pointed. Both wolves and coyotes have lots of sharp teeth.

FLOSS

Super Senses

Wolves are **predators**. That means they hunt other animals for food. Wolves are powerful hunters. They are the top predator in many habitats.

Wolves use their super senses to help them find food. They have very good eyesight, and can see tiny movements—even in the dark. A wolf also has very good hearing, and a powerful sense of smell. Their big ears catch sounds from far away. A wolf's sense of smell is almost 100 times better than a human's.

Now You Know!

The wolf does not have many animals who prey on it. This means it is at the top of the food chain in many locations. Humans are the wolf's greatest threat.

Wolf hunting

Coyotes also have sharp senses. They hear and see very well, even in the dark. A coyote also has a great sense of smell.

Coyotes are predators, just like wolves. They will catch and kill small animals. Sometimes coyotes will hunt in pairs. This allows them to catch bigger **prey**.

However, coyotes are also **scavengers**. They will eat dead animals. They will eat garbage left by people as well. Coyotes will eat berries and other fruit. Wolves only eat meat.

Wolf eating its prey

Coyote searching for prey

Now You Know!

Both wolves and coyotes are **nocturnal,** or active at night.

Howling Hellos

Both wolves and coyotes are known for their loud howls. Wolves and coyotes howl to talk to each other. A howl can mean "Hello, I am here!" Or it can mean "Danger!" or "This is my territory, go away!"

A wolf's howl is louder and deeper than a coyote's. Wolf packs often howl together. A coyote's howl is made up of yips and barks. Like wolves, coyotes howl to talk to other members of their pack, or to other coyotes who might be nearby.

Legs and Tails

Both wolves and coyotes have powerful legs. They can run very fast. A coyote's legs are long and thin. A coyote can run up to 40 miles an hour (64 km/h). It sprints, or runs quickly over a short distance before it stops.

A wolf's legs are bigger and heavier than a coyote's. A wolf can also sprint up to 40 miles an hour. However, wolves can run much longer distances on their strong legs.

Both coyotes and wolves have long, bushy tails. A coyote's tail points down while it runs. A wolf holds its tail up.

Arctic wolf running in the snow

Coyote running after prey

Where is Home?

Coyotes live all over North America. Long ago, they only lived in the deserts and grasslands in the central and southwestern parts of the United States and Mexico. Over the years, coyotes spread north into Alaska and Canada. They spread south deeper into Mexico.

Coyotes can adapt to almost any home. They live in deserts and grasslands. They live in forests and mountains. They can even live in the frozen **tundra**. Coyotes also make their homes in cities and towns. Many cities have a large population of coyotes. They may live in city parks.

The desert is home for this coyote

This coyote lives in a suburb of Chicago

These wolves
live near a lake

North
America

Europe

Asia

Africa

South
America

Australia

Antarctica

Wolves   Coyotes

Like coyotes, wolves can live in many different **habitats**. Some wolves live in the tundra. Others live in deserts or forests. Wolves are found in the northern part of North America and most of Asia. There are some wolves in Europe as well.

While coyotes can live in cities, wolves cannot. Wolves like to live in the wilderness, far away from people. Many people don't want to live near wolves. They are afraid the wolves will kill their animals or create danger to their family.

Life in the Pack

Wolves live in large groups called packs. A pack is a family group that includes six or more members. Some wolf packs are very large. Each pack has its own territory. They hunt together to kill their prey. A pack of wolves can catch and kill large animals like deer and even moose.

Each pack has a male leader and a female leader. These wolves are called the alpha male and the alpha female. The alpha wolves are the strongest wolves in the pack. All the other wolves have to follow them.

Power Word: Alpha is the first letter of the ancient Greek alphabet and is used to mean number 1 or the first of something. An alpha male/female is the #1 of a pack.

Now You Know!

An alpha male and female usually stay together for life. They are usually the only wolves in the pack that have pups.

Coyotes also live in packs. Like wolves, a coyote pack includes an alpha male and an alpha female and their family members. The size of the pack usually depends on how much food is in their territory. The more food there is, the larger the pack will be.

Coyotes live in packs, but they do not hunt in large groups. Coyotes usually hunt alone. Sometimes two coyotes will hunt together. This is an important way that coyotes are different from wolves.

Litters of Pups

Like all mammals, wolves and coyotes give birth to live pups. Both wolves and coyotes give birth to **litters** of babies called pups. A wolf usually gives birth to five or six pups. A coyote's litter is usually five or six, but can be as large as eight pups.

Wolves and coyotes keep their pups safe in a den. Mothers nurse their pups with milk from their bodies. When the pups are old enough, the parents teach them how to hunt. When the pups grow up, they might become part of the pack. Or a wolf or coyote may leave to start his own pack when he is two or three years old.

Coyote pup greeting mom

Wolf pups with their mother

Saving Wolves and Coyotes

Wolves and coyotes do not always get along with people. Many people fear these animals. They worry that wolves and coyotes might attack them, or attack their farm animals and pets.

While coyotes can live almost everywhere, wolves need lots of space away from people. Over the years, wolf habitats have been destroyed. Many kinds of wolves are **endangered**.

Today, many people are working to save this beautiful animal. Laws have been made to protect wolves. Special parks let wolves live safely in the wild.

Wolves and coyotes are important predators. They help keep nature in balance. Both animals are important parts of our natural world.

Wolf in Yellowstone National Park

Glossary

canine having to do with dogs

domesticated tamed

endangered in danger of dying out

habitats natural places where animals and plants live

litters groups of babies born at the same time

nocturnal active mainly at night

predators animals that hunt other animals for food

prey animals that are hunted by other animals for food

scavengers animals that eat dead animals or garbage

species groups into which animals and plants are divided

tundra an area in the Arctic where the ground is always frozen

Read More in the Library

Hirsch, Rebecca E. *Gray Wolves: Howling Pack Mammals.* Lerner, 2015.

Niver, Heather M. Moore. *Coyotes After Dark.* Enslow, 2016.